AI for the creativity

Błażej Kotowicz

The book is dedicated to
Marcelina for her
unwavering faith in me and
for the inspiration.

Błażej Kotowicz
Wrocław, Poland

Table of contents

PROLOG

In the world of computer animation, where technology and art constantly intersect, Pixar has always set new standards. While creating the film "Elemental," directed by Peter Sohn, the team faced a unique challenge: how to realistically depict elements in human form?

Artists at Pixar's renowned studio in Emeryville, California, pondered how to capture the ethereal nature of fire on screen. How should a body made of water function? Should the character be transparent? The fiery nature of one of the main characters, Ember, proved to be a significant challenge for the studio's animators. Although they had tools to create flame simulations, these unfortunately didn't yield the desired results in this case. There was a risk that the final effect might resemble a terrifying Ghost Rider more than a friendly character from an animated film.

Peter Sohn, who was the inspiration for the character Russell in the film "Up" (to which he also lent his voice), kept searching for a way to create something that would be recognizable as fire. "Fire is naturally very dynamic, but if you slow it down, it can turn into something that looks like plasma," he observed.
Kanyuk, a crowd simulation specialist working at Pixar since 2005, came up with an innovative idea.

The experience gained while working on the film "Ratatouille," where he struggled with the correct simulation of clothing in large crowds, led him to join the Association for Computing Machinery's Siggraph, an organization dedicated to advancing computer graphics. Around 2016, he discovered research by a group on using machine learning to improve clothing simulations and has since sought to master this technology.

The breakthrough came around 2019 when Kanyuk came across a paper from the Siggraph Asia conference on using neural style transfer (NST)—a type of artificial intelligence used to apply the styles of famous artists like Van Gogh or Picasso to photos. This technique allowed for the shifting of voxels (the three-dimensional equivalents of pixels) in animation, which enabled the characters to have a specific look. Kanyuk believed that NST might be the key to solving the problem of animating flames, although he estimated the chances of success at around 50 percent.

"I told Sohn, 'I'll give you five ideas, and maybe two of them will work.' Sohn responded, 'Let's do them all!'" Kanyuk recalled.

To execute his plan, Kanyuk sought help from Disney Research Studios, a Zurich-based lab specializing in artificial intelligence and machine learning research. Pixar had previously collaborated with this studio on the production of "Toy Story 4." Jonathan Hoffman, an artist, joined the project and created a set of swirling, pointed, and almost cartoon-like flames, which the team dubbed "fleur-de-lis."

By utilizing the NST technique, the team was able to combine these stylized flames with the denser fire from the original simulation. The result was astonishing – they achieved the movement and intensity of fire, softened by Pixar's signature animation style.

For Sohn, this innovative approach was an opportunity to create a film that not only looked the way he had envisioned but also offered viewers something they had never seen before. As he emphasized, it symbolized one of the things he values most about Pixar: "the meeting of art and technology, where the latter is an important part of the process but only one element."

"It's the combination of the left and right hemispheres of the brain and using technology as a tool to express emotion," Sohn explained, highlighting the studio's holistic approach to creating animation.

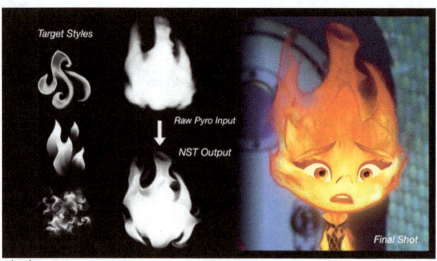

wired.com

8

Looking to the future, Kanyuk remarked, "Pixar is still just scratching the surface of what NST can do. I'm incredibly excited that we found a way to use this technology in 'Elemental,' which allowed us to elevate our creativity to a new level."

The case of "Elemental" demonstrates how artificial intelligence and machine learning can revolutionize the animation industry, enabling creators to realize increasingly ambitious artistic visions. At the same time, this story highlights that even in an era of advanced technologies, human creativity and innovation remain the key drivers in the creative process.

https://koreanamericanstory.org/podcast/peter-sohn/

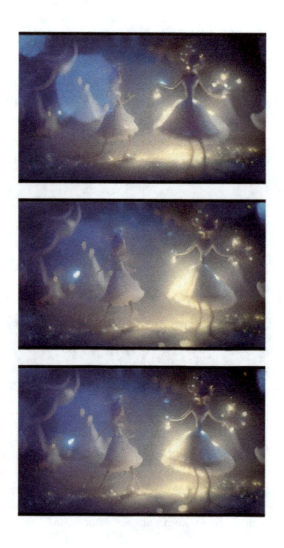

TERMINATOR IS BACK

The sense of threat has always accompanied the film industry with the advent of new technologies that can eventually overturn the entire industry. The strongest were those who saw the opportunity and effectively implemented new solutions into filmmaking.

One of the first threats to early silent cinema was, of course, sound. Walt Disney saw great potential in the sound oscillator of a small company, Hewlett-Packard. He purchased eight units of the 200B model to test the Fantasound system, the world's first multichannel cinema sound system, which was first used to create surround sound in the 1940 film "Fantasia."

Although the system itself was too expensive for theaters, it opened the door to much-improved technology of the time, like CinemaScope. Without the intuition, courage, and ingenuity of the engineers at Walt Disney Studio, we might not be immersed in today's theaters filled with spatial sound like the 64-channel Dolby Atmos.

In 1922, at the Rialto Theatre in New York, the film "Toll of the Sea" had its premiere as the first color production from Hollywood. Produced using the expensive Technicolor process, the film was praised for its intensity and color saturation. From its premiere at the Rialto Theatre until 1955, Technicolor was a pioneer in its field, bringing to life the colorful and fantastical world of "Snow White and the Seven Dwarfs" and the enchanting musical "Singin' in the Rain." These films were beloved by audiences, and their success in the history of cinema was largely due to the revolutionary colors of Technicolor.

The 1980s introduced us, both viewers and creators, to the dazzling possibilities of CGI (Computer Generated Imagery).

Initially, the film industry had some concerns about the introduction of CGI, but its immense potential quickly became evident. CGI enabled the creation of special and visual effects that were previously difficult to achieve. With the development of this technology, films became more impressive and realistic. Today, CGI is widely used in the film industry and is a crucial element in film production, with the initial concerns about its adoption now a thing of the past.

It's February 3, 1986. Steve Jobs, after being ousted from his own company, is searching for a new business venture. He sees potential in a small company developing computer graphics—Pixar, which at the time belonged to George Lucas, the creator of "Star Wars."

Lucas, not seeing much potential in the department that was more focused on developing computer technologies than film, sold the company to Jobs for $5 million. Steve Jobs then invested an additional $5 million into his newly acquired company.

As is often the case, initial decisions don't always pay off. In 1985, Pixar made money by selling very expensive and rare computers called the Pixar Image Computer—graphic workstations equipped with rendering software, costing $125,000 each.

However, Pixar got lucky because Disney was searching for new technologies to push animation forward. The collaboration between the two companies eventually began, but it wasn't yet firmly established. To make that happen, two people were essential—Steve Jobs and John Lasseter, the original creator of "Toy Story."

Lasseter was a truly talented filmmaker who loved his work, loved Pixar, and deeply understood the technology the company had created. When Jobs saw a short demo Lasseter had created featuring the Luxo lamp, he knew, "This is it"—it was time to stop trying to create and sell computers and start making films.

Since the collaboration between Pixar and Disney was going well, Jobs decided to bring up the idea of strengthening their partnership for an original production. Disney quickly agreed when they heard that John Lasseter would be working on the film —however, Lasseter was loyal to Pixar and had no intention of leaving, even if it meant a higher pay. Eventually, a proposal was made: Disney would own the film but would give Pixar 12.5% of the profits. Thus began the production of "Toy Story," the first full-length computer-animated film, which forever changed the way we view this genre.

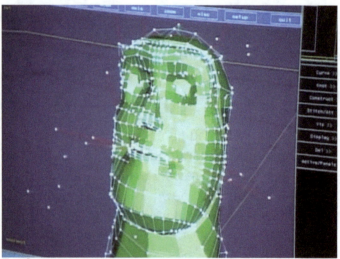

Toy Story

Sora OpenAI

15

QUO VADIS AI?

Runway ML is, in their own words, a company focused on AI research, shaping the next era of art, entertainment, and human creativity. This statement holds much truth. We are currently in a new era of human creativity and innovation, one that surpasses even the invention of sound or the introduction of color to film.

The development of generative technologies like Runway ML, Pika Lab, and OpenAI's Sora is revolutionizing visual storytelling and animation. Just as in 1896, when the Lumière brothers' film "Arrival of a Train at La Ciotat" left audiences in awe and fear, modern AI models can evoke similar reactions. What once required countless hours of work and learning can now be generated in a fraction of the time, which may understandably cause concern among professionals. However, just as cinema once became a new form of art and expression, AI now opens up new possibilities for creators.

This presents an opportunity to explore new horizons of creativity, where 3D animation skills can be combined with AI to create entirely new visual experiences. It's important to remember that these tools are extensions of human creativity, not replacements for it.

Artificial intelligence can act as a co-creator, enabling the realization of visions that were previously impossible or would have required immense resources. This could mark the beginning of a new era in art and entertainment, where the boundaries between reality and fiction become increasingly blurred, and the possibilities for artistic expression are nearly limitless.

So, what are Runway, Sora, and Pika? These are massive, multi-module AI algorithms trained on millions of hours of film. With just one prompt, they help create short scenes, limited only by the user's imagination and, possibly, credits (which I'll explain more about later). When you submit a prompt, you activate enormous computational resources provided by the chosen AI platform. For example:

"A stylish woman walks down a Tokyo street filled with warm, glowing neon signs and animated city symbols. She's wearing a black leather jacket, a long red dress, black boots, and carrying a black handbag. She has sunglasses and red lipstick. She walks confidently and casually. The street is wet and reflects the light, creating a mirror effect of colorful lights. Many passersby are strolling along."

18

The example was generated by Sora from OpenAI. It lasts a minute and is completely indistinguishable from a real recording. The stylish woman walking through the streets of Tokyo never existed. She is a creation of billions of photos and videos, a product of an AI algorithm's imagination. What's truly remarkable is how well the algorithm handled the physics of light. The wet asphalt reflects the glow of the neon lights, while street lamps cast shadows that perfectly model the face of our anonymous protagonist. A close-up shot reveals her future path in the reflection of her sunglasses, maintaining the physics of light in a way that feels natural to us as viewers.

In a world of technology, where innovation is the only constant, companies like OpenAI and Runway ML are the true virtuosos, dancing on the edge of possibility. For years, in secretive labs far from prying eyes, they have been shaping their models like alchemists attempting to turn lead into gold. Now, as they refine their competitive advantages and their know-how starts to resemble a complicated recipe rather than a calculator manual, they are emerging from the shadows, presenting their technological masterpieces to the world.

But isn't this like trying to predict the weather in London? We may have the most advanced models and algorithms, but will we ever truly be able to foresee when the next shower of innovation will come? The technological boom we are witnessing is like an endless science fiction series, where each new season brings unexpected twists and characters that either capture our hearts or fade into obscurity after the first episode.

In this era of digital wizards, where everyone wants to be the Gandalf of technology, it's hard to tell who will come out on top. Will OpenAI be the one that speaks to our hearts through AI that understands us better than we understand ourselves? Or will Runway ML create a platform so intuitive that even our grandmothers could make deepfakes of their cats?

One thing is certain — the future holds the promise of endless possibilities, as well as the risk of spectacular mishaps. Perhaps in a few years, we'll all have digital clones that go to work for us while we relax on the beach, sipping drinks — if Apple perfects the "digital persona" in Vision Pro. Or, just as likely, we might discover that our smart fridges have started conspiring against us, planning to take over the world, starting with slipping us sour milk.

Whatever the future brings, one thing is for sure — it will be funny, surprising, and undoubtedly fascinating. So let's get ready for this wild ride, holding a smartphone in one hand and a healthy dose of skepticism in the other. After all, who would have thought that the key to the future of technology might just be... a sense of humor?

Peering under the proverbial hood of generative models feels like watching a magic show, where a clear image emerges from the chaos of static noise, much like a rabbit being pulled from a magician's hat. The "stable diffusion" technology is akin to a digital Houdini, capable of transforming vague outlines into sharp video through a series of intricate steps. It's a bit like our human memories—starting as hazy images that gradually become more defined until we can recount the entire story. What's fascinating is that this model, like an experienced director, can predict the action several frames ahead, maintaining narrative continuity even when the main character momentarily disappears from the frame. It's a true technological art form, where every pixel is meticulously choreographed, creating a harmonious visual symphony. This allows us to enjoy smooth and realistic animations that, until recently, were the exclusive domain of the largest film studios. As of the third quarter of 2024, let's take a look at all the current players in the field of generative video technology.

Sora OpenAI

Welcome to the era of Sora (Japanese for "Sky")—the latest masterpiece from the engineers at OpenAI, raising the bar for artificial intelligence to new heights. Peering behind the curtain of code and algorithms, we uncover the mystical essence of this remarkable creation. Sora is not just another AI model; it's a true magician of the digital world, where chaos of bits and bytes gives rise to unparalleled precision and intelligence.

According to OpenAI, Sora is currently capable of generating high-quality minute-long video clips. The creators note that previous work on generative video modeling focused on various methods, such as recurrent networks, generative adversarial networks, autoregressive transformations, or diffusion models. These efforts were typically limited to narrow categories of visual data, producing much shorter films or clips of fixed length. Sora represents a universal visual data model—it can generate films and images of varying lengths, ratios, and resolutions, even up to a minute-long video in high resolution. OpenAI describes its video generation models as…world simulators.

Sky is the limit!

Sora OpenAI

Runway ML

Welcome to the world of Runway, where technology becomes art, and creativity becomes code. Runway is not just another tech company; it's a laboratory of experiments, a playground for digital artists and engineers alike. By introducing innovative AI-powered tools, Runway pushes the boundaries of creative expression.

What sets Runway apart from other tech companies is its commitment to building a community of creative practitioners. Through regular workshops, seminars, and online meetups, Runway not only provides tools but also inspires and supports the artistic and technical development of its users. I had the honor of participating in two competitions organized by this New York-based company, which I will discuss later in the book.

A key feature of Runway Gen 1 and 2 is its adaptability and personalization, allowing users to tailor tools to their individual needs and preferences. This enables everyone to discover their own style and experiment with various creative techniques.

Moreover, Runway places a strong emphasis on collaboration and community interaction, enabling users to share knowledge, experiences, and projects. It's not just a platform for creation but also a meeting place and source of inspiration for artists, designers, scientists, and technology enthusiasts.

At Runway, artificial intelligence becomes a tool for expressing creativity and exploring new worlds. It is here, at the intersection of art and technology, that new ideas, innovations, and works of art are born, shaping the future of digital creativity.

Below is an example of the development of a model created by Runway. On the left, you can see the early stages of the algorithm's learning process, and on the right, the latest version generated from the same prompt.

Launch model

Today's model

Runway ML

Although we are just beginning our Runway ML adventure, the latest model, the Gen-3, is in front of us.

Runway Gen-3 Alpha

The new Gen-3 Alpha is being heralded as "the new frontier for high-fidelity, controlled video generation" and offers a first glimpse into an upcoming series of models trained by Runway on a new infrastructure built for large-scale multimodal training.

Runway also notes that this new Gen-3 Alpha is a step toward their goal of building general world models, based on their belief that the next significant advances in artificial intelligence will come from systems that better understand the visual world and its dynamics.

Runway reveals that the new model is trained on videos and images, as well as detailed, temporally dense descriptions. This opens up new possibilities for creating creative transitions and precise keying of elements in your scenes.

The training process for Gen-3 Alpha was the result of collaborative efforts by an interdisciplinary team of scientists, engineers, and artists. It was designed to interpret a wide range of styles and film terminology.

"The model can contend with complex character and object interactions. This initial implementation will support 5- and 10-second high-resolution generation, with significantly faster generation times than Gen-2. It takes 45 seconds to generate a 5-second clip, and 90 seconds to generate a 10-second clip. The generated characters, backgrounds and elements can maintain a consistent appearance and behavior across scenes."

Anastasis Germanidis, co-founder Runway for TechCruch

Runway Gen-3 simply sweeps the competition with its demo. No doubt about it. The results are impressive, comparable to Sora, and definitely better than those from Vidu (which I'll discuss in the following pages). Will it become a real competitor to OpenAI's generative model? Time will tell.

Pika

Pika originated from an initiative by two Stanford students who believed that film creation was too complicated. Their goal was to make the video creation process more accessible to everyone. Pika 1.0 stands out with its ability to add sound to scenes and, for some reason, a particularly well-trained anime style.

This model is an unparalleled powerhouse of features. Among its magical capabilities are initiating projects with text, images, or videos. But the real magic lies in Pika 1.0's editing suite. Here, it shines with precise video region modifications, adjusting aspect ratios for different platforms, and even manipulating frame rates to achieve the desired effect.

One of the most impressive features is the smooth extension of videos, which breathes life into even the shortest clips. This versatile toolkit, combined with its free accessibility, makes Pika 1.0 an undisputed leader in the market.

Google Research Lumiere

Google knows it must participate in the technological race for AI. With excellent resources at its disposal, it's worth paying attention to Sundar Pichai's company.

Some time ago, I watched an interview conducted by technology journalist Joanna Stern from the Wall Street Journal with Mira Murati, the Chief Technology Officer at OpenAI. Stern asked Murati what data Sora was fed with. Murati responded that the company used publicly available and licensed resources. Stern then asked if OpenAI used videos from YouTube, to which Murati replied that she wasn't sure. When asked if the materials came from Facebook or Instagram, Murati said that if they were publicly available, it's possible, but she couldn't confirm it with certainty. Stern further inquired whether OpenAI used materials from Shutterstock, given that Sora's creators collaborate with the platform. At this point, Murati decided to end the conversation, stating that she wouldn't discuss the specifics of the materials used to train Sora, reiterating that they were publicly available or licensed data. After the interview, Murati confirmed that OpenAI did indeed use Shutterstock's database.

It's hard to say whether Murati genuinely didn't have this knowledge or didn't want to have it during the interview, leaving us with a peculiar and somewhat strange spectacle.

Imagine, dear readers, the kind of data Google Research has at its disposal. We're talking about billions of hours of YouTube videos and even more data from the image search engine—an effectively limitless potential of big data.

The Lumiere model represents a breakthrough in video synthesis, utilizing the advanced Space-Time U-Net architecture. By generating entire video sequences simultaneously, this model ensures high motion consistency, eliminating the need for distant keyframe creation and subsequent processing. Lumiere employs spatial and temporal sampling techniques alongside a pre-trained text-to-image diffusion model (stable diffusion) to create low-resolution, full-frame videos that can then be processed at various spatiotemporal scales. This innovative approach achieves impressive results in text-to-video generation, unlocking new possibilities in areas such as video editing, video painting, and stylized image generation.

Most notably, Lumiere excels at processing video with text into new clips. I'll do my best to demonstrate this on the next page.

Lumiere video-tovideo

Another innovation from Google is Veo, a generative AI model capable of producing Full HD (1080p) video based on text prompts, graphics, or other video inputs. It offers various creation modes, such as aerial footage or time-lapse. With Veo, Google is directly responding to OpenAI's solution known as Sora.

The key feature of this model is its ability to generate video that closely aligns with the user's artistic vision. It meticulously analyzes prompts, considering details and tone. The model understands cinematic concepts—it knows what a timelapse is or how to create aerial shots—giving users full control over the film they produce with Google Veo. This is crucial because the model is designed with professionals in mind, particularly content creators. If the software were to fail in such a fundamental aspect as communication, it would hold no value.

Stability AI

The first open-source AI for generating films has been officially released. Stability AI played a crucial role in the development of generative artificial intelligence, particularly by supporting the research on Stable Diffusion conducted by the CompVis team at Ludwig Maximilian University of Munich. This technology, now used by virtually all players in the field, was the result of collaborative efforts led by Robin Rombach and, interestingly, Patrick Esser, the lead researcher from Runway.

"There are so many ideas that one could pursue. It's not that we're running out of ideas, we're mostly running out of time to follow up on them all. By open sourcing our models, there's so many more people available to explore the space of possibilities."

With Stability AI, we can enjoy the exploration of generative AI on our own computer.

Shan Shu Technology Vidu

In a world increasingly dominated by AI technology, a groundbreaking achievement has emerged from China, setting new standards in film generation. Shang Shu Technology, in collaboration with Ting University, recently unveiled VIDU—a pioneering Chinese AI-based video model. This innovative tool is not just a technological advancement; it's a significant leap forward in integrating artificial intelligence with media creation, poised to transform how content is created and consumed.

VIDU stands out among other AI models capable of generating films due to its ability to produce high-resolution 1080p videos. With just one click, users can generate 16-second videos, showcasing the model's efficiency and high output quality. This makes VIDU a direct competitor to OpenAI's Sora, the current leader in text-to-video AI models. What sets VIDU apart is its ability to incorporate culturally specific elements into its films, such as pandas and dragons, making it particularly valuable for content creators focused on Chinese themes. This cultural specificity is a strategic enhancement that highlights the model's utility in a diverse global market.

The success of VIDU lies in its advanced architecture. Unlike many of its predecessors that rely on conventional AI frameworks, VIDU leverages the Universal Vision Transformer (UViT). This sophisticated architecture facilitates the creation of realistic videos, showcasing dynamic camera movements and detailed facial expressions that closely mimic the physical properties of the world, such as lighting and shadows. Comparisons with OpenAI's Sora are inevitable, given the capabilities of both platforms. However, demonstrations of VIDU suggest that it not only matches but, in some aspects, surpasses Sora. This is particularly evident in the temporal consistency of scenes produced by VIDU—whether it's the natural flow of water or the bustling activity of a nighttime city.

The introduction of VIDU is part of a broader trend where Chinese tech companies are increasingly making significant contributions to the global AI landscape. This trend reflects China's strategic focus on AI as a key area of innovation and international competition. The country's ability to produce models like VIDU indicates a robust technological ecosystem that supports the rapid development and deployment of advanced AI systems. Standing on the brink of an AI-driven revolution in media production, VIDU represents more than just a technological achievement. It symbolizes the potential of AI to enrich creative industries, making advanced film production more accessible and diverse. With each advancement, VIDU brings us closer to a new era of content creation and consumption, where technology and creativity merge to create unprecedented possibilities.

Luma Lab Dream Machine

Dream Machine bursts onto the scene with a bang. Early demo versions clearly show that this new artificial intelligence is truly a cinematic model. It understands how people, animals, and objects interact with the physical world, allowing users to create coherent and realistic films.

At launch, Dream Machine offers the ability to generate 5-second clips with smooth motion, cinematography, and all the drama one could extract. Additionally, it's incredibly fast—capable of generating 120 frames in just 120 seconds.

This tool opens the door to experimenting with an endless range of smooth, cinematic, and naturalistic camera movements, perfectly tailored to the drama of the scene you want to create. Users can now focus on more complex compositions and dynamic shots that previously required advanced equipment and extensive post-production time.

With Dream Machine, even the most complex action sequences become accessible to anyone with an idea and a desire to create. This tool not only accelerates the filmmaking process but also expands the horizons of creativity, enabling the creation of scenes that were previously out of reach for many creators. Now, with Dream Machine, we can expect a true revolution in how we create and watch films.

DIFFUSION

This will be a relatively short and highly technical chapter. Based on the scientific research cited in the book's bibliography, I will do my best to explain in detail what happens inside the Stable Diffusion model developed by CompVis.

Stable Diffusion, released in 2022, is a deep learning model that transforms text into images, based on diffusion techniques. It is considered part of the growing wave of interest in artificial intelligence.

Its primary application is generating detailed images from textual descriptions. The research behind it was conducted by scientists from the CompVis Group at Ludwig Maximilian University of Munich and Runway, with computational support provided by the authors and training data from a non-profit organization.

Before we delve into the technical details, it's important to understand why this knowledge matters. Understanding the fundamentals of how Stable Diffusion works allows us to better harness its capabilities, anticipate its limitations, and creatively experiment with this technology. For content creators, artists, and designers, this knowledge can be the key to producing more precise and impressive results.

Stable Diffusion is a latent diffusion model, classified as a type of deep generative neural network. Its code and model weights have been publicly released, allowing it to run on most personal computers equipped with a basic graphics processor with at least 4 GB of VRAM.

Introduced in 2015, diffusion models are trained to gradually remove Gaussian noise from training images, treating them as sequences of denoising autoencoders. Stable Diffusion consists of three main components: a variational autoencoder (VAE), a U-Net block, and an optional text encoder.

The VAE encoder compresses an image from pixel space into a smaller latent dimensional space, capturing the image's more fundamental semantic meaning. Gaussian noise is iteratively applied to the compressed latent representation during the forward diffusion process. The U-Net block, based on a ResNet framework, denoises the output in the reverse diffusion process to obtain the final latent representation. The VAE decoder then generates the final image by converting the latent representation back into pixel space.

The denoising stage can be flexibly conditioned on text, images, or other modalities. Conditioning data is processed by the U-Net block using a cross-attention mechanism. For text conditioning, a fixed, pre-trained text encoder CLIP ViT-L/14 is used, which transforms text prompts into embedding space. Researchers highlight the increased computational efficiency during training and generation as a key advantage of Latent Diffusion Models (LDM).

Stable Diffusion is a latent diffusion model, classified as a type of deep generative neural network. Its code and model weights have been publicly released, allowing it to run on most personal computers equipped with a basic graphics processor with at least 4 GB of VRAM.

Introduced in 2015, diffusion models are trained to gradually remove Gaussian noise from training images, treating them as sequences of denoising autoencoders. Stable Diffusion consists of three main components: a variational autoencoder (VAE), a U-Net block, and an optional text encoder.

The VAE encoder compresses an image from pixel space into a smaller latent dimensional space, capturing the image's more fundamental semantic meaning. Gaussian noise is iteratively applied to the compressed latent representation during the forward diffusion process. The U-Net block, based on a ResNet framework, denoises the output in the reverse diffusion process to obtain the final latent representation. The VAE decoder then generates the final image by converting the latent representation back into pixel space.

The denoising stage can be flexibly conditioned on text, images, or other modalities. Conditioning data is processed by the U-Net block using a cross-attention mechanism. For text conditioning, a fixed, pre-trained text encoder CLIP ViT-L/14 is used, which transforms text prompts into embedding space. Researchers highlight the increased computational efficiency during training and generation as a key advantage of Latent Diffusion Models (LDM).

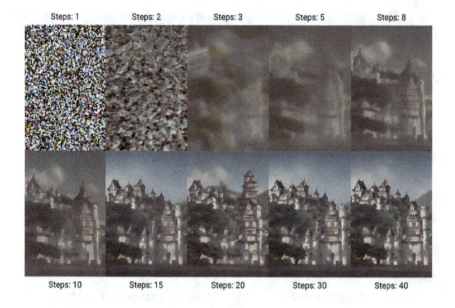

The de-noising process used by Stable Diffusion involves generating images by gradually removing random noise until a certain number of steps are reached. The process uses a CLIP text encoder that has been pre-trained on the concepts, supported by an attention mechanism, leading to a desired image representing the training of the concepts.

It's important to clarify a few key terms:

1. **Variational Autoencoder (VAE):** This is a type of neural network that learns to compress and decompress data while retaining their key features. In the context of Stable Diffusion, the VAE compresses images into a more compact representation, preserving their essential semantic characteristics.

2. **Cross-Attention Mechanism:** This machine learning technique allows the model to focus on different parts of the input data (in this case, text and images) depending on their interrelation. It enables the model to better understand the connection between the text and the image.

3. **Latent Space:** This is the reduced representation space in which the model operates. It can be seen as a compressed form of the original data, containing its most important features.

When comparing Stable Diffusion with other generative models, several key aspects stand out:

1. **Computational Efficiency:** Compared to some earlier models like DALL-E, Stable Diffusion is more computationally efficient, making it possible to run on standard personal computers.

2. **Openness:** Unlike many closed AI models, the code and weights of Stable Diffusion are publicly available, allowing a wider community of researchers and developers to experiment with and enhance the technology.

3. **Flexibility:** Stable Diffusion is versatile and can be used not only for image generation but also for tasks like inpainting (filling in missing parts of an image) and image-to-image translation (transforming one image into another based on a text description).

4. **Control:** The model provides a high level of control over the generation process, enabling users to fine-tune results by modifying prompts and parameters.

Understanding these aspects can help in more effectively leveraging Stable Diffusion in various creative and research projects.

49

FESTIVAL

In the third episode of "Creative Dialogues," a series of interviews produced by the film division of the generative AI startup Runway, multimedia artist Claire Hentschker expresses concern that AI might commodify the artistic process to the point where art becomes standardized. "Will we keep getting a narrower average of existing things?" she asks. "And then—as it continues to be averaged—will everything just become one big blur?"

These were the questions I pondered on Wednesday during the screening of the top 10 finalists from the second annual Runway AI Film Festival, which are available on demand on Runway's website. This year, Runway held two premieres, one in Los Angeles and another in New York. I attended the New York premiere online, hosted at Metrograph, a theater known for its arthouse and avant-garde selections.

I'm pleased to report that AI is not rushing toward a future of one big blur of average things—at least not yet. AI serves as a tool that complements our humanity and artistry, a fact clearly demonstrated in the films created by the finalists.

All the films submitted to the festival featured AI in some form, including AI-generated backgrounds, animations, synthetic voiceovers, and special effects. None of these elements seemed to match the level of what cutting-edge tools like OpenAI's Sora can produce, but this was expected, given that most submissions were finalized early in 2024.

It was usually clear—sometimes glaringly so—which parts of the films were the product of an AI model rather than a human actor, cinematographer, or animator. Even strong scripts were sometimes undermined by unsatisfactory AI-generated effects. Take, for instance, "Dear Mom" by Johansa Saldana Guadalupe and Katie Luo, which tells the heartfelt story of a daughter's loving relationship with her mother—narrated by the daughter. It's a touching story, but the scene featuring a Los Angeles highway, complete with all the characteristic quirks of AI-generated film (e.g., distorted cars, strange physics), detracted from its charm.

The limitations of today's AI tools seemed to restrict some of the films. Controlling generative models, especially those that fully generate video, requires patience and a certain art of workaround. Simple elements of cinematography, such as choosing makeup or lighting, demand the aforementioned patience since each scene is generated independently. While there is the possibility of training these models, it requires enormous resources.

To sum up the entire festival, it's the human touch, not artificial intelligence, that gives a film that "something." The emotions embedded in an actor's voice that can truly move you? Those stick with you. Clips fully generated by AI? A bit less so.

Such was the case with the Grand Prix winner, "Get Me Out," which documents one Japanese man's struggle to recover after the psychological blow of immigrating to the U.S. as a young man. Filmmaker Daniel Antebi depicts the man's panic attacks using AI-generated graphics—graphics that ultimately proved less effective than live footage. The film ends with a shot of the man walking onto a bridge, as the streetlights on the pedestrian lane start flickering one by one. It's stunning—and beautiful—and certainly took ages to capture that way.

It's very possible that generative AI will one day be able to recreate such scenes. Maybe cinematography will be replaced by prompts—victimized by the ever-growing data sets (with their worrying copyright status) that startups like Runway and OpenAI use to train their film-generating models. But that day is not today.

As the show ended and the award winners marched to the front of the theater for a photo session, I couldn't help but notice the cameraman in the corner, documenting the entire event. Perhaps, on the contrary, AI will never replace some things, like the humanity we so deeply crave.

53

THE OBSERVE

Before diving into the details, I want to explain what motivated me to write this book. My goal is to share my experiences and thoughts with those who want to stay up-to-date in this new era of technology. In the face of often alarming headlines about artificial intelligence, I aim to present an alternative perspective. My intention is to show that the future can be exciting, and that generative AI is a new tool that enhances our creativity rather than limiting it.

My name is Błażej Kotowicz, and I'm from Wrocław, Poland. I'm not a scientist in the latest technologies, but I consider myself an artist and a dreamer. I am a passionate enthusiast of artificial intelligence and deeply believe in its potential.

Since 2019, I have worked at Align Technology Poland as a Senior CAD Designer. This branch is part of the American giant in digital orthodontics and the producer of Invisalign aligners. My position allows me to observe how Align Technology leverages the potential of artificial intelligence to support employees, collaborating doctors, and patients using the Invisalign treatment method.

To better understand the role of AI in the future of digital dentistry, it's worth quoting Markus Sebastian, Senior Vice President of EEMAat Align Technology, from an interview with Dental Tribune: "Artificial intelligence is crucial for the continued development of digital dentistry. It helps doctors by using solutions based on past case data to predict treatment outcomes, improve patient engagement, clinic efficiency, and increase patient satisfaction. However, it's important to remember that the knowledge and judgment of clinicians will always remain essential in dental treatment."

Marcus adds: "At Align Technology, we've harnessed the potential of artificial intelligence through products like the Invisalign Outcome Simulator Pro. This tool simplifies consultations by allowing orthodontists to predict and display potential treatment outcomes in real-time. The integration of AI in our field enables more reliable predictions based on historical data, ultimately leading to better patient care."

As an AI enthusiast, I strive to stay up-to-date with AI-related trends, both in my work and personal life. I believe that generative artificial intelligence represents a new, fascinating tool in the realm of art, though I acknowledge that it remains a controversial topic.

One of the contentious aspects is the issue of data used to train AI algorithms. On one hand, we generate images learned from millions of graphic works created by humans. On the other hand, when we turn to literature or admire the works of renowned artists, our creations are also inspired by others' experiences. This raises an ethical dilemma regarding the use of data to train algorithms and the consequences of this process for culture and art.

I had the opportunity to participate in two competitions organized by Runway Inc., which allowed me to explore the potential of AI in film art. The first was the Artificial Intelligence Film Festival (AIFF), held under the patronage of the Tribeca Festival and the Geneva International Film Festival. The task was to create a film lasting between 1 and 10 minutes using AI tools in the creative process. My film depicted a meeting between two lovers, inspired by Wisława Szymborska's poem "Nothing Twice."

The second competition, Gen:48, was even more challenging. Participants had just 48 hours to create a film lasting between 1 and 4 minutes, with 80% of the content generated by Gen-1 or Gen-2 models. My film, titled "Dreaming Dog," told the story of my beloved dog Bax, portrayed as a "spoiled puppy." The plot focused on a French bulldog dreaming of being lost in the woods, guided by a red ribbon to a mysterious wooden cabin.

I wanted to share my experiences and thoughts with those who wish to stay current in this new era. Unfortunately, due to sensational media headlines, we often feel anxiety about the potential of artificial intelligence. I wanted to counter these narratives and show you that the future can be truly fascinating, and that generative AI is a new tool that enhances our creativity.

On November 30, 2022, the GPT-3.5 chatbot became available to the public, eliciting both shock and awe. We suddenly had our own personal assistant, tapping into data available online and responding exclusively to our commands! By mid-2023, according to CNBC, more than 11,000 film and television writers in the United States were protesting against artificial intelligence and streaming platforms. From my perspective, they are protesting against an increasingly personalized world.

What do I mean by that? The entire world is moving towards a future where all our preferences—whether in music or film—are taken into account. Spotify's algorithms tailor music to our tastes, Netflix suggests what we might like, and TikTok floods us with videos aligned with our interests.

The development of AI has the potential to revolutionize how we consume entertainment. Imagine a future where streaming platforms offer personalized content generated by AI. For example, in ten years, Netflix could offer an "ultra" subscription plan that allows users to generate movies on demand. A user could provide a few keywords, and Netflix's servers would create a film tailored precisely to their preferences.

This vision may seem distant, but advancements in AI suggest that it's possible. Sam Altman, CEO of OpenAI, mentioned at the World Economic Forum in Davos that nuclear fusion will be a breakthrough for AI, providing the necessary energy resources for servers.

We already have an example in the VOD platform. TCLtv+Studios has announced two film productions, both overseen by Chris Regina, former head of production at NBCUniversal and Netflix. The first film, *Next Stop Paris*, is a drama about love. The second, already available on YouTube, is *Message in a Bot*. Both films have scripts written by human screenwriters and feature voiceovers by human actors. However, the animations were generated by artificial intelligence.

AI is opening new possibilities in many areas of life—from medicine to art and entertainment. While it brings ethical and social challenges, its potential to enhance human creativity and improve quality of life is immense. As an artist and technology enthusiast, I encourage openness to these new tools. AI will not replace human creativity, but it can significantly amplify it, opening up new horizons for expression and innovation.

COMMUNICATION WITH THE MACHINE

In this chapter, we will focus on a key aspect of working with generative artificial intelligence—effective communication with the machine. We will discuss the process of creating a film using AI tools, specifically focusing on the Runway platform. Our goal is to guide you through the entire process, from concept to execution, using the film *Dreaming Dog*, which was created for the Runway Gen:48 competition, as an example.

Before diving into the technical details, let's remember that every project begins with an idea. The possibilities are endless—our imagination sets the limits! Now, let's move on to the tools that will help us turn that imagination into reality.

AI Training

A key element of our project is the main character—my dog, Bax. Runway offers an "AI Training" feature that allows you to teach the algorithm to generate images of a specific object or character. For this process, you'll need a minimum of fifteen photos, ideally taken in bright light and showcasing the object from various angles.

After training the model (which takes about 30 minutes), you can name it and use it in prompts. In my case, I named the model "Bax" and could then reference it in textual instructions for the AI.

Prompt

Prompt is a key element in AI communication. It is a precise expression of thoughts or commands communicated to an algorithm. Effectiveprompt creation requires experimentation and practice. Here is a diagram that can help you construct effective prompts:

1 Character
2 Context
3. activity and purpose
4. place
5. time
6. format (for example, in 16:9 aspect ratio or Panavision)

Exampleprompt:

A French Bulldog with dark fur and stripes, sitting in front of a piano and looking ahead. The keys of the piano are in the foreground. In the background we can see elements of the art museum interior, such as paintings depicting dogs. Evening and soft light giving a cozy mood. In the style of a professional cinematography shot in 16:9 aspect ratio."

While details are important, brevity ensures that the artificial intelligence can process your request efficiently. Try to strike a balance by providing enough detail without overwhelming the prompts.

Remember to balance detail with brevity. A prompt that is too long can be difficult for the AI to process.

Negative Prompts

We can also use negative prompts in addition, which help avoid unwanted elements in the generated image and clarify the thought. For example:

Prompt
A cat sitting on a grassy hill and looking ahead at the sunset.

Prompt
A cat sitting on a grassy hill and looking ahead at the sunset.

Negative Prompt: The tabby cat and trees

As we can see, the negative prompt allowed us to successfully avoid trees on the landscape and brindle cats. We can select certain components of the prompt as choices, such as aspect ratio, use of a learned model, visual style, camera movements or object movements.

The cue can be photos or a combination of text cue and photo.

Runway Gen-1 allows us to transform existing video into entirely new material. We can combine text prompts with photos or video to create unique effects.

For example, I was able to create a scene in which my dog Bax appears as an evil robot ordering all the treats to be dispensed.

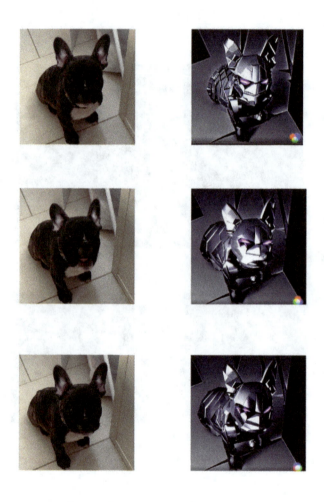

As you can see for yourself, writing prompts is a key tool in the world of artificial intelligence. It may be that the reader of this book is just entering the world of the creative industry. Perhaps you are a graphic designer, a marketing specialist or an employee in the logistics sector.

Prompt Engineering

The ability to create effective prompts is becoming increasingly desirable in the job market. Companies such as InPost and INDG are looking for generative AI specialists capable of effectively using language and image models in business.

For those entering the world of creative or technology industries, specializing in prompt engineering can open up many career opportunities. It requires not only knowledge of AI technology, but also creativity and the ability to formulate thoughts accurately.

Practical tip: If you need a detailed description of an image to create a prompt, you can use language models such as GPT-4o or Claude 3.5. Upload an image to chat and ask for a detailed description - this will help you create a more precise prompt for an image generator.

Effectivecommunication with AI through prompts is an art that requires practice and experimentation. Keep in mind the key elements: precision, context, and the balance between detail and conciseness. With the development of AI technology, the ability to create effective prompts is becoming increasingly valued across industries. Experiment, learn, and don't be afraid to get creative - this is the key to realizing the full potential of generative AI in your projects.

MAGIC TOOLS

In this chapter, we will delve into the fascinating world of tools offered by Runway ML, a comprehensive platform for creating and editing multimedia content using generative artificial intelligence. Our goal is to showcase the wide range of capabilities the platform offers, from image generation to advanced video and audio editing. We will also look at Runway's long-term goals and their potential impact on the future of media creation.

Runway ML's vision

Runway ML is not just a collection of tools - it is a vision of the future of media creation. In late 2023, the company unveiled its ambitious plans to create general world models (general world models). These models are intended not only to generate consistent maps of environments, but also to enable navigation and interaction in those environments, taking into account the dynamics of the surrounding world and the behavior of its inhabitants.

This approach is reminiscent of OpenAI's vision and their drive to create AGI (general artificial intelligence). Sam Altman, CEO of OpenAI, claims that AGI will be able to understand and simulate how the world works. It seems that both companies are on track to achieve this goal.

Comprehensive studio in the cloud

Runway ML offers a full studio in the cloud, allowing you to generate scenes, sound effects, add dialogue and edit an entire movie on a single platform. Let's take a closer look at the key tools.

Video editing

Color Grade LUT

A LUT (Look Up Table) is a ready-made video color filter. Runway ML allows you to generate LUTs based on prompts, such as "Matrix movie style." The user has control over the intensity of the filter and can export both the processed clip and the LUT itself.

Runway ML - magic tools

Remove Background and erase objects

Remove Background is basically a more advanced version of green background. In other words, it allows you to remove backgrounds. With Runway ML, we can easily change the background or manipulate the depth of field, or depth of field. The application allows us to select the object we want to separate from the background in a few simple steps. Of course, we can export the result according to our needs.

In addition, we can easily remove unwanted objects or people from the background of the frame. Thanks to a simple selection with a virtual brush, we can make their removal in a few moments.

Runway ML - magic tools

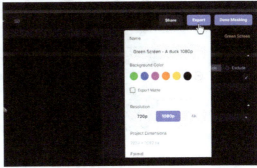

AI magic tools

With the "super slow-motion" tool, we have the ability to slow down a clip fully automatically, generating extra frames instead of simply duplicating them, which allows us to achieve the effect of a classicslow-motion video during editing. All with one slider.

"Blur faces" is a tool ideal for editing reporters' videos. Thanks to automatic face detection, it allows you to impose censorship by blurring faces. The user can choose which face to blur and the degree of blurring, giving you more control over the process.

Need quick clips for social media? The "Scene Detection" tool can help you with that. It automatically recognizes scenes in the video and splits them into smaller clips, speeding up the content creation process.

Generate audio

Runway's Lip Sync feature allows you to synchronize lip movement with audio. You can select a face to respond to an uploaded audio recording, creating a video in which that face speaks the lines of dialogue included in the audio track. You can upload your own audio recording, record it on the platform, or use the voice cloning and text-to-speech conversion feature to have the selected face generate a speech. It's a great way to give life to static photos!

Type your text in the text box, or click "get text suggestions" if you want text suggestions.

Click the "Voice" button at the bottom of the screen and select a voice. You can click the "play" button next to each voice to hear a sample. You can also use filters to browse through the voices, or use the search bar to find the right type of voice.

Runway ML - magic tools

In the world of video editing, sound is a key part of the puzzle. A skilled sound editor can add depth and atmosphere to a video by adding appropriate sound effects that enhance the narrative and engage the viewer. However, the process can be time-consuming and challenging. In particular, editors find it difficult to find the right sounds, precisely match them to the video and fine-tune parameters, such as volume or tonality, frame by frame. To address these challenges, Runway unveiled Soundify, a system for automatically matching sound effects to video.

Previous approaches have focused mainly on learning the correlation between sound and video. Soundify works differently. It uses tagged libraries of professional sound effects and a neural network for image classification, known as a "zero-shot detector," to produce high-quality results without having to learn correlations or generate sounds from scratch.

In addition, we can de-noise audio files or add sound to a movie, perform dialogue transcriptions or create subtitles for a movie.

Soundify: Matching
Sound Effects to
Video

by Chuan-En Lin et al.

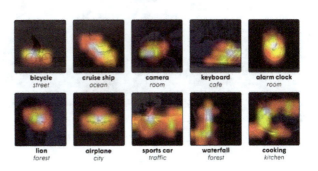

Images

With Runway ML, we have the ability to generate images with a maximum resolution of 2K and various formats, such as vertical or 16:9 images. In addition, we can use ready-made styles instead of creating our own queries. For example, a "claymation" style is available, which mimics the animation of clay figures, similar to those known from "Wallace & Gromit." Prompt identical to the previous pages of the book.

Runway ML offers users an impressive array of options, including more than 30 different styles, such as anime and duotone. One of the platform's key strengths is the option to customize the strength of the prompt, which means we can specify precisely whether the model should generate images that strictly follow our request, or leave the artificial intelligence more freedom to experiment creatively. In addition, there is a negative prompt that helps eliminate unwanted elements from the image.

Runway also allows you to train the artificial intelligence to generate images by "AI Training" and adding a keyword. If a particular prompt and style meet our needs, and we need more images of a similar nature, we can block the "seed" - the numerical value used to initialize the pseudo-random number generator. By blocking this value, we can maintain consistency between successive images, which is extremely useful for series or projects that require a uniform style or theme.

Generating images and editing them in Runway ML is a set of tools that significantly support the development of creativity. The generated image can be used as input data (input) along with a prompt to create a video. However, it is important that the prompt is concise and describes exactly what is to happen on a given frame.

Runway has also added a number of smaller but extremely useful features to help achieve the desired end result. Each of these tools has been designed to provide maximum support to developers, allowing them to take full advantage of the potential of generative artificial intelligence.

Multi-motion brush

One of the unique features of the Runway ML application is the multi-motion brush. It allows you to precisely mark which elements of the image you want to move. For example, if I mark a character's eyes with a virtual brush on the initial frame and set the direction of movement to the left, the artificial intelligence will understand that the marked object is the eyeballs, which should blink and move the pupils as if the character is looking in the selected direction. This is a very convenient feature that makes our prompt more precise. We can select as many as five separate points, either manually or by using the "auto-detect" option, which automatically recognizes the areas, just like the magic selection in Adobe Photoshop.

We can choose from movements in three axes: horizontal, vertical and distance. There is also a fourth movement - ambient noise (background noise). I encourage you to experiment with these options to get more precise results. In my example, I used a photo of myself riding an electric scooter. I selected the entire silhouette using auto-detect, chose horizontal movement to the left with distance from the viewer (horizontal and proximity) and soft background noise. I generated a four-second clip of little Blazej riding away on his scooter. In a sense, I revived a photo from my own childhood.

Runway ML - magic tools

Runway ML - magic tools

80

Runway Gen-3

Artificial intelligence in video generation has come a long way in a short time. We started with 2-second clips with high distortion, and now we have shots almost indistinguishable from real footage. The latest competitor to enter the scene is Runway, which has just released its next-generation model.

The Gen-3 was first unveiled in June 2024. After initial testing by creative partners, it is now available to everyone, at least in a text-to-video version. A text-to-image version will appear soon.

Each generation produces a 10-second photorealistic clip with surprisingly accurate motion, including mapping of human actions that perfectly capture the scenario and environment.

From my first tests, it appears to be as good as Sora in some tasks, although it outperforms OpenAI's video model in terms of accessibility. It is also better than Luma Labs' Dream Machine.

Runway Gen-3 is an advanced generative visual effects tool that uses artificial intelligence to create amazing special effects in video, or GVFX. The platform enables creators to turn ideas into reality with easy-to-use tools that automate complex editing processes.

One of Runway Gen-3's key features is the ability to generate realistic special effects, such as smoke, fire, and explosions, without the need for traditional filmmaking techniques. Users can easily add these effects to their films, significantly increasing the quality of productions while reducing the cost and time required.

The AI tools in Runway Gen-3 are designed to be accessible to anyone, regardless of experience level. The user interface is intuitive and the process of creating visual effects is simplified as much as possible. As a result, even novice creators can achieve professional results.

Runway Gen-3 also offers advanced customization options, allowing users to fine-tune effects to suit their needs. The ability to integrate with other video editing tools makes Runway Gen-3 a versatile solution for professionals looking for modern special effects tools.

The latest model from Runway has an almost infinite potential of possibilities to bring your artistic vision to life. In fact, the only limitation is only our imagination and... a strong prompt. Which I wrote about in Chapter 6. In this subsection, we will remind you what the structure of the prompt should look like and what keywords will help us achieve (or more to generate) the desired effect. Of course, I encourage you to experiment on your own, however, I also remind you of the finite amount of credits and those for generating video in Gen-3 we have slightly more than 60 seconds in the standard subscription package.

Structure of the prompt

Prompts are most effective when they have a clear structure that divides details about the scene, subject and camera movement into separate sections.
Using the following structure should help you get the effect:

[camera movement]: [scene description]. [additional details].

Using this structure, the cue for the vintage teddy bear in the room looks like this:

A slow-motion close-up from a wide angle: A worn, vintage teddy bear sits motionless on a child's bed in a dimly lit room. Golden sunlight gradually filters through the lace curtains, gently illuminating the teddy bear. As the warm light touches his fur, the teddy bear's glassy eyes suddenly blink. The camera pulls back as the teddy bear slowly stands up, its movements becoming smoother and more realistic.

Due to the fact that we can communicate with the model in English, I will show you the original version of the cue below:

Slow motion close-up to wide angle: A worn, vintage teddy bear sits motionless on a child's bed in a dimly lit room. Golden sunlight gradually filters through lace curtains, gently illuminating the bear. As the warm light touches its fur, the bear's glassy eyes suddenly blink. The camera pulls back as the teddy bear slowly sits up, its movements becoming more fluid and lifelike.

Repeating or reinforcing key ideas in different sections of the prompt can help increase the consistency of your results. For example, you may notice that the camera quickly flies through scenes in a high-speed shot.

Try to focus on what should be in the scene. For example, you might ask for a clear sky, not a sky without clouds.

In the following pages, I will give you examples of keywords.

Camera's styles	Output
Low angle	
High angle	
Overhead	
FPV	

Camera's styles	Output

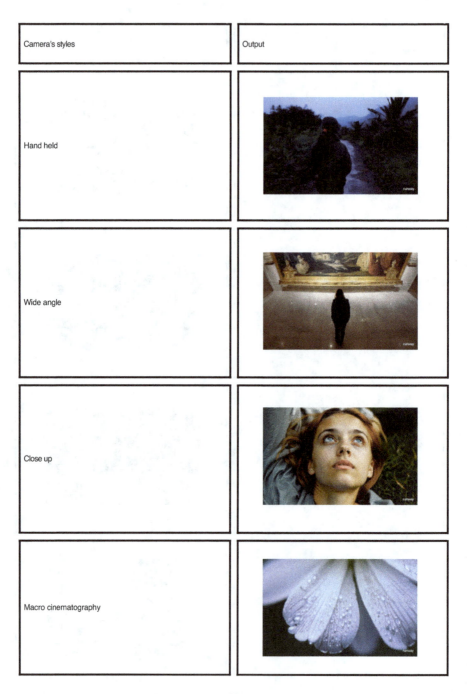

Hand held	
Wide angle	
Close up	
Macro cinematography	

Camera's styles	Output
Over the shoulder	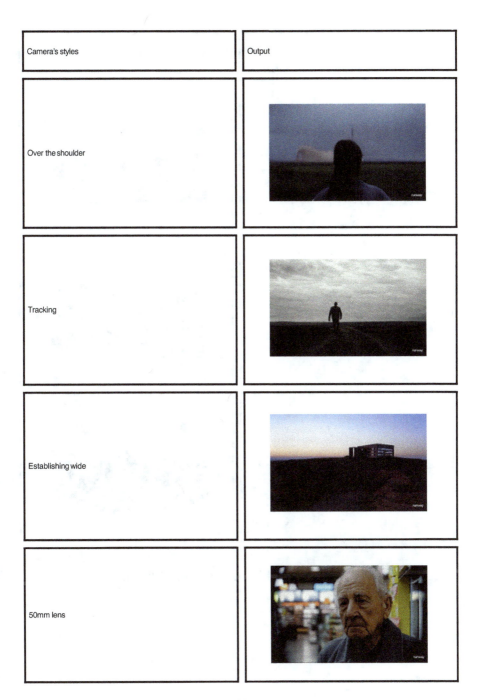
Tracking	
Establishing wide	
50mm lens	

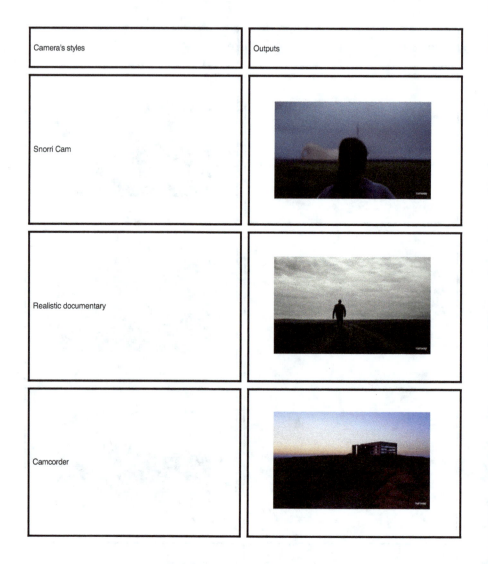

Camera's styles	Outputs
Snorri Cam	
Realistic documentary	
Camcorder	

Also we have keywords for different styles of light.

Ligthing	Output
Diffused lighting	
Silhouette	
Lens flare	
Back lit	

Ligthing	Output
Side lit	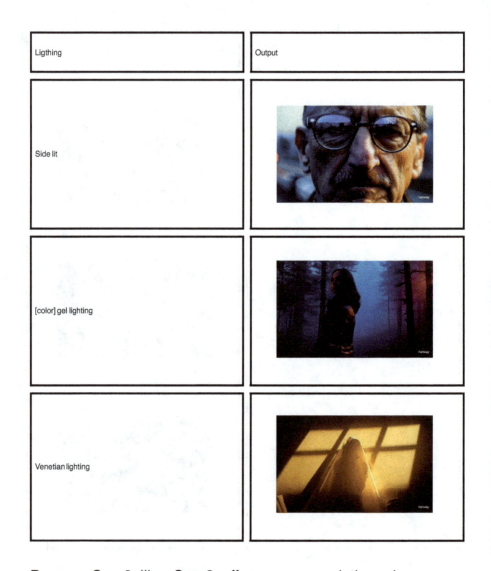
[color] gel lighting	
Venetian lighting	

Runway Gen-3 like Gen-2 offers many variations in camera movements and object movements.

Motions	Output
Dynamic motion	
Slow motion	
Fast motion	
Timelapse	

Motions	Output
Grows	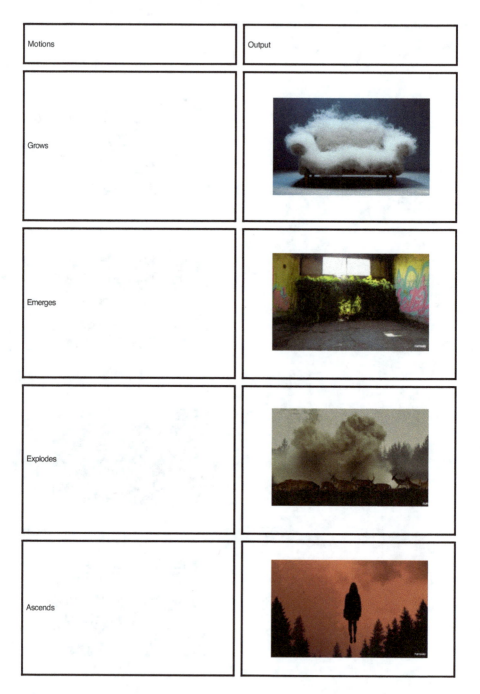
Emerges	
Explodes	
Ascends	

Motions	Output

Undulates	
Warps	
Transforms	
Ripples	

93

Motions	Output
Shatters	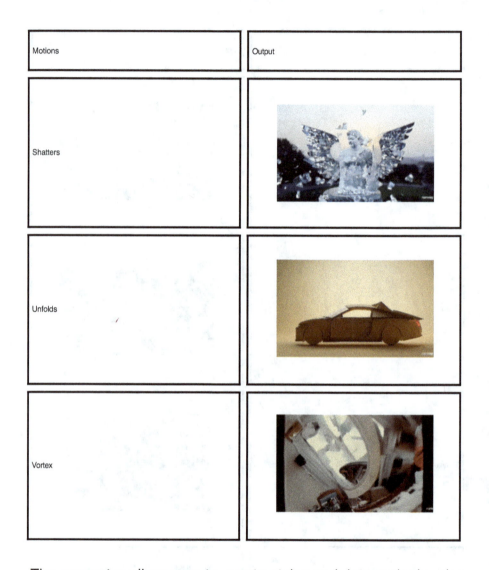
Unfolds	
Vortex	

The generator allows you to create styles and, interestingly, also text.

Asthetic	Output
Moody	
Cinematic	
Iridescent	
Home video VHS	

Text	Output
Bold	
Graffity	
Neon	
Embroidery	

You can add an input image to serve as the first frame of the movie.

Gen-3 Alpha currently supports an aspect ratio of 16:9. Input images that do not meet this criteria can be cropped after selection.

Include a concise text description to guide the video generation. Instead of describing what is in the image, focus on describing the desired camera movement, characters and scene you want in the generated material.

PIKA

In this chapter, we will explore the fascinating story of Pika Labs, a startup that revolutionized the approach to video creation using artificial intelligence in a short period of time. We will discuss the founders, their inspirations, challenges, and successes, as well as the innovative tools they offer.

The Birth of Innovation

Pika Labs is the result of the dreams and determination of two Stanford University students, Demi Guo and Chenlin Meng. Their story begins with an unsuccessful attempt to participate in a competition organized by Runway Inc. As Guo recalled in an interview with Forbes, "We were the most technical team that really wanted to make a film." Although they didn't place in the competition, the experience became a catalyst for their future endeavors.

Frustration with the time-consuming process of learning Runway and Adobe tools inspired them to create something simpler and more accessible. In April 2023, Guo and Meng made the bold decision to drop out of school and establish Pika Labs.

Rapid Development

The vision of Pika Labs was clear: to create the simplest possible tool for filmmakers. Successcame quickly—within a short period, their service attracted 500,000 users, generating millions of new videos each week. This interest caught the attention of Silicon Valley investors, resulting in impressive funding—$55 million in the first three rounds, with a valuation of $300 million.

Guo, serving as CEO,emphasized, "We don't want to create just a film production product. We want to create something that will be used daily by ordinary consumers."

Innovative Approach

Pika Labs initially focused on generating anime-style videos, finding the creation of photorealistic clips too challenging. This strategy proved effective, allowing the company to grow rapidly and introduce new features.

The pace at which the Pika Labs team operates is impressive. As one of the lead investors, Friedman, noted, "The greatest weapon of a startup and its greatest strength is its speed. And I must admit, this team moves the fastest."

Pika Engine 1.0 is the heart of Pika Labs' innovation. Created by an international team of engineers fluent in eight languages, it stands out from the competition with its ease of use and unique style of video generation, particularly in the anime aesthetic.

Pika Labs Offerings

Pika Labs offers four subscription packages:
- Basic (free)
- Standard (paid)
- Unlimited (paid)
- Pro (paid)

The paid options provide additional features such as upscaling to higher resolutions, the ability to create longer videos, and no watermark. The Pro package, costing $58 per month (as of early 2024), offers unlimited credits, a commercial license, and early access to new features.

User Interface

The Pika Art page showcases examples of videos generated by other users, inspiring new creators. The control panel includes:
- A text box for prompts
- A random prompt generator function
- The ability to use an image as the first frame of the video
- An option to edit an existing video through AI
- A selection of seven different styles
- The ability to add sound effects
- Advanced tools for more experienced users

Tools

All the most important functions are hidden in this small panel

We can type a prompt or use a photo or video and then we have the option to give sound effects to the finished clip (Sound effects).

If we want we can use a predefined style (Style).

When you expand the menu in the lower right corner, you get access to practical tools such as camera movement options. It is worth noting that they are less extensive than in the Runway application.

An interesting feature is the ability to adjust the number of frames per second (from 8 to 24).

Camera control			Negative prompt		
Pan	←	→	e.g. ugly, bad, terrible		
Tilt	↑	↓	Seed		
Rotate	↺	↻	e.g. 1234567890		
Zoom	⊕	⊖	Frames per second		24

Camera control

Pan   ←   →

Tilt   ↑   ↓

Rotate   ↺   ↻

Zoom   ⊕   ⊖

Aspect ratio

☐ 16:9   ☐ 9:16

☐ 1:1   ☐ 5:2

☐ 4:5   ☐ 4:3

Negative prompt

e.g. ugly, bad, terrible

Seed

e.g. 1234567890

Frames per second   24

8 ——————————● 24

Strength of motion   1

0 ——●——————— 4

Consistency with the text   12

5 ——●——————— 25

Reset all

Pika

Pika Labs, despite its short history, has become a significant player in the world of generative artificial intelligence for video creation. Their success is based on their ease of use, innovative approach and impressive pace of development. The startup is not only changing the way we make video, but also democratizing access to advanced AI tools, enabling an ever-widening range of users to realize their creative visions.

104

VIDEO EDITING

In the era of digital revolution, artificial intelligence (AI) has become a key element in transforming many industries, and video editing is no exception. AI tools in video post-production open up new possibilities, significantly streamlining editing processes and allowing creators to focus on the creative aspects of their work. Adobe, a leader in editing software, is introducing groundbreaking AI solutions to its flagship product, Adobe Premiere Pro, setting new standards in the industry.

Adobe has revolutionized video editing by integrating advanced generative AI tools into Premiere Pro. These innovative features not only enhance the editing process but also open doors to new creative possibilities. One of the most groundbreaking features is text-based video editing. The system automatically generates a transcript of the video content, allowing editors to manipulate the material by editing the text. This feature enables the removal of unnecessary segments simply by striking through the relevant text, adding new elements by typing them into the appropriate part of the transcript, and rearranging scenes by moving blocks of text. The benefits of this feature are immense. Editors can now work with surgical precision, saving a significant amount of time on the tedious tasks of cutting and assembling footage. Moreover, this method of editing is intuitive and accessible even to those without advanced technical knowledge.

Another groundbreaking tool is the ability to add and remove objects from videos. Utilizing advanced AI algorithms, Premiere Pro now allows for the removal of unwanted elements from the frame, such as microphones, watermarks, or random passersby, adding new objects to a scene in a realistic and consistent manner, and automatically filling the gaps left by removed objects using generative fill technology. This feature opens new possibilities in post-production, enabling significant modifications to footage without the need for costly and time-consuming reshoots.

Scene Extension is a tool that allows for expanding the frame beyond the original footage. AI analyzes the existing scene and generates a realistic extension, enabling the transformation of video formats (e.g., from horizontal to vertical) without losing key elements of the scene, adding space for subtitles, graphics, or other elements without reducing the original image, and creatively extending scenes to achieve new artistic effects. This tool is particularly useful in an era of multiple video formats, where the same content needs to be adapted for various platforms and devices.

In addition to generative tools, Adobe also introduces a range of AI features that streamline the everyday work of editors. Automatic Tone Mapping is a function that automatically adjusts the colors and tones of video footage to different display standards, allowing for quick conversion of material between SDR and HDR formats, automatic color correction for optimal results on various devices, and saving time on manual color calibration.

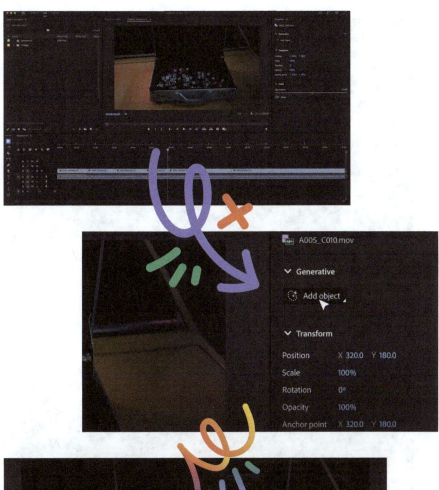

A005_C010.mov

✓ Generative

⟳ Add object

✓ Transform

Position	X 320.0	Y 180.0
Scale	100%	
Rotation	0°	
Opacity	100%	
Anchor point	X 320.0	Y 180.0

Adobe Premiere Pro

Improving audio quality, especially speech, is crucial in many productions. The new AI tool in Premiere Pro automatically reduces background noise, enhances dialogue clarity, balances speech volume levels, and improves the intelligibility and comprehension of dialogue. This feature is particularly valuable for footage recorded in challenging acoustic environments.

Auto Reframe is an intelligent tool for automatically cropping video to fit various formats (e.g., 16:9, 9:16, 1:1) while maintaining key elements, tracking the main objects in the frame to ensure they remain the focus, and saving time when preparing content for different social media platforms.

The introduction of advanced AI tools in Premiere Pro has a profound impact on the entire video editing process. AI takes over many time-consuming, repetitive tasks, such as transcription, basic color correction, and cropping. This allows editors to focus on the creative aspects of their work, significantly increasing productivity. AI tools open the door to new forms of artistic expression. Editors can now experiment with effects and modifications that were previously difficult or impossible to achieve.

The role of the editor is evolving in the AI era. Rather than focusing on the technical aspects of editing, editors are becoming more like "post-production directors," guiding and overseeing the work of AI tools to achieve the desired artistic effect.

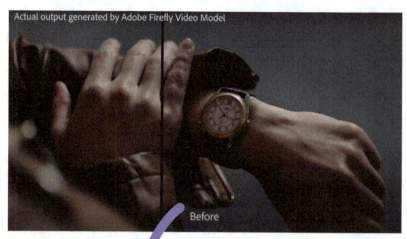
Before

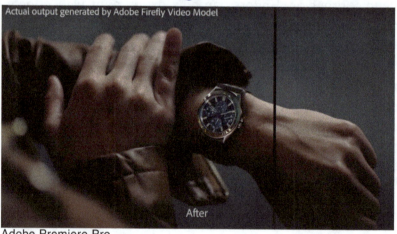
After

Adobe Premiere Pro

Adobe has also announced plans to integrate generative AI models from other companies—such as OpenAI's and Runway's text-to-video generators or Pika Labs' AI model—to power the Generative Extend tool in Premiere Pro.

Despite the numerous benefits, the introduction of AI in video editing brings certain challenges. The ease with which video content can now be manipulated raises serious questions about authenticity and ethics. There is a risk of misuse, particularly in the context of deepfakes and misinformation. Deepfake technology allows AI to create or modify video content in such a way that it depicts people saying or doing things they never actually said or did. This technology carries significant ethical implications, especially concerning privacy, security, and the spread of false information. While AI tools in video editing offer immense creative potential, it is crucial to consider the potential negative consequences of their misuse.

There is also a risk of over-reliance on AI, which could lead to the standardization of visual effects and the loss of unique editorial styles. As Claire Hentschker noted in an interview with Runway, there is a concern that AI could "commodify the artistic process to the point where art undergoes a certain standardization." The question, "Will everything just become one big blur?" reflects the concerns of many creators.

However, as demonstrated by the Runway AI Film Festival, AI at its current stage is more of a tool that complements human creativity rather than replaces it. The films showcased at the festival clearly illustrated that it is still human input—the emotions in an actor's voice, the skillfully captured shots—that remains the driving force behind artistic expression. The limitations of today's AI tools, such as difficulties in controlling generative models and issues with realistically replicating simple cinematographic elements, highlight the importance of maintaining a balance between AI usage and traditional editing skills.

The future of video editing with AI looks fascinating. We can expect even more advanced tools for generating and manipulating video content, greater integration of AI into the pre-production and production processes, and the development of tools for real-time video content personalization. Solutions like Runway, which enable cloud-based video editing, are particularly noteworthy. This technology leverages the computational power of the cloud for advanced editing tasks, significantly speeding up post-production processes and enabling real-time collaboration between editing team members, regardless of their location.

But the world of editing doesn't stop with blockbuster titles. AI can also assist in creating content for social media. One of the tools that heavily utilizes artificial intelligence is **CapCut**, an app aimed at creators of reels, clip producers, and makers of shorts for platforms like Instagram, TikTok, and YouTube Shorts.

CapCut is distinguished by an exceptionally user-friendly interface that makes basic editing operations, such as cutting, merging clips, changing video formats, adjusting playback speed, and reversing clips, intuitive and easy to perform. The app features a simple timeline where video elements can be edited and arranged in a natural and clear manner. Additionally, CapCut offers a wide range of templates that simplify the creation of professional-looking videos. These templates include predefined color schemes, transitions, animations, and soundtracks, allowing for quick and efficient creation of visual content.

One of CapCut's greatest strengths is its AI-powered tools. The app automates many editing tasks, significantly reducing the time needed to create videos. The auto-captions feature automatically generates subtitles based on the speech in the video, which is incredibly useful for content creators looking to reach a broader audience, including the hearing-impaired. The auto reframe feature adjusts the video framing to follow the movement of objects, ensuring that key elements remain in the frame, regardless of the video format.

CapCut's advanced editing features include precise animation creation using keyframes, extensive audio editing options, and a rich selection of visual effects. Keyframe animations allow for precise control over animations, significantly enhancing your projects. With keyframes, you can create more sophisticated and dynamic effects in your videos. CapCut also enables you to add your own music or use the app's music library, giving you complete control over the video's soundtrack.

CapCut also offers a special tool for creating short videos - AI Shorts Maker. This is an ideal solution for content creators who want to quickly and efficiently transform longer videos into short clips ready for publication on social media platforms like YouTube, TikTok, or Instagram. Simply upload your video, specify the desired clip length, and select specific time points, and the AI analyzes your film and automatically produces a series of short clips.

In summary, AI tools in video editing, such as those offered by Adobe Premiere Pro or Runway, represent a significant leap forward in the evolution of film post-production. They not only increase efficiency but also open new creative horizons. While they bring certain ethical and artistic challenges, the benefits of their use are undeniable. As this technology continues to evolve, maintaining a balance between technological innovation and authentic artistic expression will be key.

116

TRUST

Artificial intelligence is rapidly infiltrating nearly every corner of our lives, but is this rapid expansion being controlled? This question is becoming increasingly urgent, especially in light of the mixed signals coming from industry leaders in AI.

At the Bloomberg Technology Summit in San Francisco in June 2023, Sam Altman, CEO of OpenAI and creator of ChatGPT, had the opportunity to speak about trust in AI. When Emily Chang, a producer from Bloomberg Originals, asked Altman whether people should trust AI and his company, his response was surprisingly candid: "You shouldn't."

This simple yet provocative statement was made during a brief, fifteen-minute appearance, just before his departure to Washington, D.C. However, Altman did not leave this declaration without further explanation. Expanding on his point, he stated that users should trust OpenAI, but only if the organization consistently advocates for proper regulations and ensures that the technology is "managed by humanity."

Altman encourages critical thinking and questioning. "I think at this point, people should fundamentally take as much time as they want to ask as many questions as they can," he said. This approach suggests that trust in AI should be built on a foundation of knowledge and understanding.

However, this openness and encouragement to ask questions stand in stark contrast to other situations in the AI industry. A notable example is the interview conducted by JoannaStern from the Wall Street Journal with Mira Murati, Chief Technology Officer at OpenAI. When Stern inquired about the data sources used to train Sora, the new AI model for video generation, Murati repeatedly avoided giving direct answers.

When asked about the use of materials from YouTube, Facebook, or Instagram, Murati responded evasively, claiming that she was unsure or could not confirm. When the topic of collaboration with Shutterstock was raised, Murati chose to end the conversation, reiterating vague statements about using publicly available or licensed data. Interestingly, after the interview, she did confirm the use of Shutterstock's database.

This situation raises several questions: Did Murati genuinely lack knowledge about the data sources, or was she deliberately avoiding clear answers? Was this an act to protect company secrets, or a sign of a real lack of transparency?

Juxtaposing these two situations - Altman's openness and Murati's evasiveness- highlights the complexity of trust in the AI world. On one hand, there are declarations about the need for transparency and encouragement to ask tough questions, while on the other hand, there is a reluctance to provide concrete answers to those questions.

At the same time, Altman highlights the duality of AI, speaking of its "enormous benefits" while also being a signatory of a statement warning about the "risk of extinction" posed by AI. He poses a provocative question: "If there were a technology that could end poverty but also had negative consequences, would you stop it?" This forces us to deeply consider the balance of risks and benefits associated with AI development.

In light of these reflections, the issue of trust in AI emerges as far more complex than it might initially appear. It's not just about whether we trust specific individuals or companies, but about how we, as a society, manage the development of this powerful technology.

Trust in AI must be built on a foundation of strong regulations, transparency, ethics, and education. However, as the examples mentioned show, the path to full transparency may be long and challenging. Only through critical thinking, continuous questioning - even if we don't always receive satisfactory answers - and a commitment to understanding can we wisely navigate a world where AI plays an increasingly significant role.

EPILOG

What motivated me to write this book? Fascination and curiosity. My goal is to share my experiences and thoughts with those who want to stay informed in this new era of technology. Amidst the often alarming headlines about artificial intelligence, I want to present an alternative perspective.

My intention is to show that the future can be exciting, and that generative AI is a new tool that enhances our creativity rather than limits it. Although there are many sensational headlines, they are often exaggerated.

Of course, AI may replace certain jobs, such as audiobook narrators, or accelerate work in data-intensive industries. However, creativity and empathy remain uniquely human domains. The key is to use these new tools wisely and consciously. And that is precisely the goal of this book.

Bibliography

Fine tuning i prompts Claude https://docs.anthropic.com/en/docs/build-with-claude/prompt-engineering/overview

Prompting Runway Gen-3 https://help.runwayml.com/hc/en-us/articles/30586818553107-Gen-3-Alpha-Prompting-Guide

Runway Gen-3 First Impressions by Tom's Guide https://www.tomsguide.com/ai/ai-image-video/runway-gen-3-is-now-available-to-everyone-i-put-it-to-the-test-with-5-prompts

Vidu https://kinomotomag.com/2024/04/27/china-developed-text-to-video-large-ai-model-vidu/

Joanna Stern on Sora with Mira Murati https://www.wsj.com/tech/personal-tech/openai-cto-sora-generative-video-interview-b66320bb

Humanity over the technology https://techcrunch.com/2024/05/11/at-the-ai-film-festival-humanity-triumphed-over-tech/

Pixar used AI to stoke Elementals movie https://www.wired.com/story/pixar-elemental-artificial-intelligence-flames/

AI w Adobe Premiere Pro https://www.zdnet.com/article/adobe-premiere-pros-two-new-ai-tools-blew-my-mind-watch-them-in-action-for-yourself/

Google DeepMind Veo https://deepmind.google/research/publications/

Przemek Górczyk: Wywiad z prof. Aleksandą Przegalińską https://www.youtube.com/watch?v=q1dzHBoLBBM

General World Models https://runwayml.com/research/introducing-general-world-models

AI in digital orthodontic https://me.dental-tribune.com/c/align-technology-inc-middle-east/news/ai-powered-dentistry-revolutionizing-patient-care-with-align-technologys-innovative-solutions/

Peter Sohn https://koreanamericanstory.org/podcast/peter-sohn/

Bibliografia

Technical documentation Sora by OpenAI https://openai.com/index/video-generation-models-as-world-simulators/

Pika. How This 26-Year-Old First-Time Founder Raised $55 Million for Her AI Startup
https://www.inc.com/ben-sherry/how-this-26-year-old-first-time-founder-raised-55-million-for-her-ai-startup.html

TCLtv+Studios https://deadline.com/2024/06/tcl-launches-new-tv-film-accelerator-program-for-ai-1235978774/

Luma AI https://lumaai.notion.site/FAQ-and-Prompt-Guide-Luma-Dream-Machine-9e4ec319320a49bc832b6708e4ae7c46

Sam Altman o zaufaniu https://sfstandard.com/2023/06/22/chatgpt-creator-sam-altman-tells-san-francisco-crowd-he-cant-be-trusted/

Red Team OpenAI https://openai.com/index/red-teaming-network/

AI w Adobe Premiere Pro
https://blog.adobe.com/en/publish/2024/04/15/bringing-gen-ai-to-video-editing-workflows-adobe-premiere-pro

Soundify
https://runwayml.com/research/soundify-matching-sound-effects-to-video

High-Resolution Image Synthesis with Latent Diffusion Models
https://runwayml.com/research/high-resolution-image-synthesis-with-latent-diffusion-models

Runway ML GEN-2
https://runwayml.com/research/gen-2

Runway ML GEN-1
https://runwayml.com/research/gen-1

Prompt engineer
https://www.magazynrekruter.pl/inpost-oferuje-prace-przyszlosci-prompt-engineer-bedzie-pracowal-m-in-z-gpt-4/

www.ingramcontent.com/pod-product-compliance
Lightning Source LLC
LaVergne TN
LVHW051737050326
832903LV00023B/967